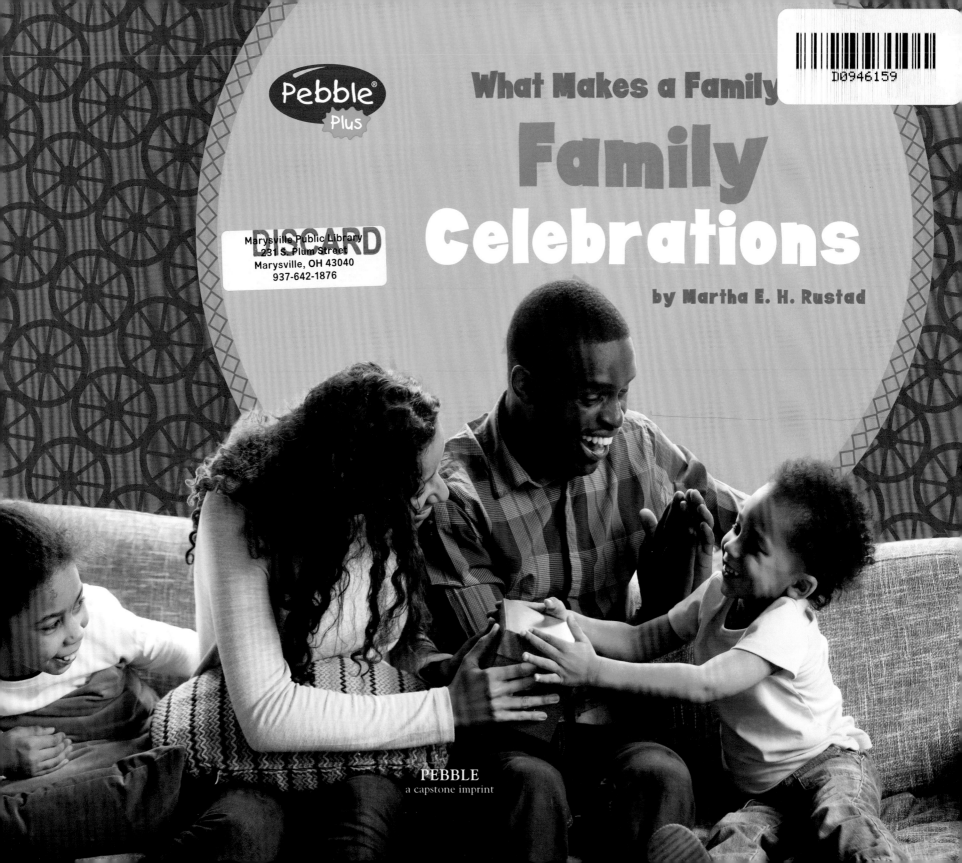

Pebble® Plus

What Makes a Family
Family
Celebrations

by Martha E. H. Rustad

PEBBLE
a capstone imprint

Little Pebble is published by Pebble
1710 Roe Crest Drive,
North Mankato, Minnesota 56003
www.mycapstone.com

Library of Congress Cataloging-in-Publication Data
Library of Congress Cataloging-in-Publication Data is available on the Library of Congress website.
ISBN 978-1-9771-0906-4 (library binding)
ISBN 978-1-9771-1049-7 (paperback)
ISBN 978-1-9771-1276-7 (eBook PDF)

Editorial Credits
Marissa Kirkman, editor; Cynthia Della-Rovere, designer;
Eric Gohl, media researcher; Tori Abraham, production specialist

Image Credits
Alamy: Eyal Nahmias, 15, Mint Images Limited, 11, Richard Ellis, 9; iStockphoto: asiseeit, 17, monkeybusinessimages, 21; Shutterstock: FamVeld, 5, fizkes, 1, Monkey Business Images, cover, 7, 13, 19
Design Elements: Shutterstock

All internet sites appearing in back matter were available and accurate when this book was sent to press.

Note to Parents and Teachers
The What Makes a Family? set supports national standards related to social studies. This book describes and illustrates ways families celebrate The images support early readers in understanding the text. The repetition of words and phrases helps early readers learn new words. This book also introduces early readers to subject-specific vocabulary words, which are defined in the Glossary section. Early readers may need assistance to read some words and to use the Table of Contents, Glossary, Read More, Internet Sites, Critical Thinking Questions, and Index sections of the book.

Printed and bound in China.
001654

Table of Contents

Celebrate!

Families celebrate together.

They honor important events.

Each family has its own way

of celebrating. Celebrations

are great parties.

Jamie's family celebrates her birthday. She turns 7 years old today. Mom wakes her up early. Dad bakes a cake. Everyone sings.

Holidays

Carolina's family celebrates the Day of the Dead. They share stories about family members who have died. Carolina's brother lights a candle.

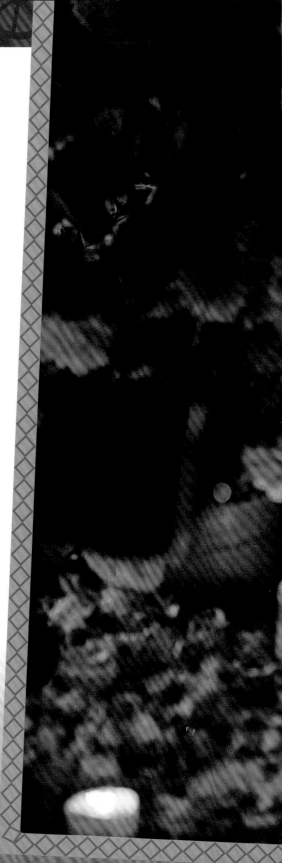

Malik's family celebrates Juneteenth. This holiday marks the end of slavery in the United States. His family has a picnic after the parade.

Other Celebrations

Haddie's family celebrates Family Day. It is the day they adopted Haddie. She and her dads remember the first time they met.

Kaya's family celebrates
a powwow. People in her
Chumash tribe gather.
They sing songs and dance.
Her grandpa plays a drum.

Simon's family celebrates
a homecoming. His mom is
home from her army job! They
really missed each other. Simon
gives his mom a hug and a kiss.

Tyler's family celebrates report card day. He and his sisters are proud of their hard work. The family eats ice cream together.

Family Fun

Gina's family celebrates game night. Gina and her brother pick a game. The whole family cheers for each other. Family celebrations are fun!

Glossary

adopt—to bring a person into your family

brother—a male sibling

celebration—a gathering with activities on a special day

grandpa—the father of a person's mother or father

holiday—a day that is meant to celebrate an event or person

homecoming—a return home

powwow—a social gathering for American Indians featuring traditional dances and music

sister—a female sibling

slavery—the owning of other people; slaves are forced to work without pay

tribe—a group of people who share the same language and way of life

Read More

Benjamin, Tina. *It's My Birthday!* Inside My World. New York: Gareth Stevens Publishing, 2015.

Bullard, Lisa. *My Family Celebrates Day of the Dead.* Holiday Time. Minneapolis: Lerner Publications, 2019.

Grack, Rachel. *Juneteenth.* Blastoff! Readers: Celebrating Holidays. Minneapolis: Bellwether Media, Inc., 2019.

Internet Sites

Day of the Dead
https://kids.nationalgeographic.com/explore/celebrations/day-of-the-dead/

Family Birthday Traditions
http://www.pbs.org/parents/birthday-parties/tips_post/family-birthday-traditions/

Juneteenth Facts and Worksheets
https://kidskonnect.com/history/juneteenth/

Critical Thinking Questions

1. How does your family celebrate birthdays?

2. Which family celebration is your favorite?

3. How can you celebrate family game night?

Index